Author Biography

Linda was born in Easington Colliery, Co Durham in 1958, and then moved to Leicester in the early 1960's, which is where she spent her childhood. But, it was in 'Shakespeare County,' Warwickshire, where she says she 'grew up' during and after completing her counseling diploma. She is now an experienced counselor, supervisor, & trainer, behavioral family therapist & author of three self help books, counseling text books, children's book and a four novels.

She is a survivor of navigating herself through her own teenage years and those of her children.

Thank you and dedications

Linda would like to thank her three children

Paul Christian Spencer

Claire Louise Violet Connor

Emma Marie Sarah Harvey

Without whom she would not have the knowledge to write this book and for the bumpy ride through their teenage years and for the lessons we all learned from this, and for the fact that we all survived this without killing each other.

!

We would also like to dedicate this book to my parents

Owen and Vera Williams

For their dedication, stamina and perseverance through my own teenage years.

Linda Mather [TEENAGERS ARE FROM PLUTO]

TEENAGERS ARE FROM PLUTO

TEN TIPS FOR PARENTING TEENAGERS

Copyright @ 2013 Linda & Michael Mather

This book contains material under International and Federal Copyright Laws and Treaties. Any unauthorised reprint or use of this material is prohibited. No part of this book may be reproduced or transmitted in any form or by any means, electronic or mechanical, recording or by any information storage or retrieval system without express written permission from the author.

However we are happy for professionals working with parents to photo-copy extracts from this book to support their work.

www.linda.mather.co.uk

ISBN-13: 978 1481834841

ISBN-10: 1481834843

Cover art by Dreamstime

Prologue

Chapter One — Acceptance that teenagers are on a different planet!

Chapter Two — Are both parents beating from the same drum?

Chapter Three — There is no such thing as the 'perfect parent!'

Chapter Four — Tough Love! Be consistent with firm boundaries!

Chapter Five — You will never be their best friend!

Chapter Six — Caring for teenagers without rescuing!

Chapter Seven — Get off that stage!

Chapter Eight — Protect your inner child!

Chapter Nine — Empathy you have got to be kidding!

Chapter Ten — Putting your plans into action

Epilogue — Taking care of yourself

> Mother Nature is providential; she gives us twelve years to develop a love for our children before turning them into teenagers!
>
> William Galvin

Prologue

> Father: "Son you really do ask a lot of questions, I'd like to know what would have happened if I'd asked as many questions when I was a boy."
>
> Teenage son: "Perhaps you would have been able to answer some of mine!"

I wish I had a pound for every time I had been asked as a therapist and as a mother:

"Linda how did you manage the teenage years" or "From a psychological point of view what advice would you give to parents raising teenagers?"

There is not a parent that I know that has swum through the teenager years of their offspring without some difficulty; it is part of the course. However from my experience if these years are managed in a healthy way then the terrible teen years end between nineteen and twenty one.

If however, they are managed in an unhealthy way then the challenging behaviours of our offspring can go on further into their twenties and sometimes early thirties. Therefore if your hard work is done between twelve and eighteen, then hopefully you will have lovely, respectful and healthy functioning adults.

> **"Teenagers are Gods punishments for having sex"**

I am a survivor of three teenage children; I am watching my own children now beginning the journey with their own teenagers. Karma comes to mind! I say survivor because it does feel like a survival of the fittest at times. I am also a therapist with a good understanding of human behaviour, therefore I decided that I have enough knowledge and experience to write this book.

I have the experience of joint parenting, being single parents and of being a step parent to teenage children. And I have lived to tell the tale!

One of the first thing I thought about when starting this book was if there was one resource that was of the most importance needed when raising teenagers, what would it be, and my answer is:

A SENSE OF HUMOUR

This is why I decided to run humour through my book, with jokes and comical quotes as it is, I felt an important tool to have in your survival kit. However I hope that it looks at the serious side to teenage difficulties too.

I would also like to make a point that all teenagers have wonderful, pleasant, caring and comical sides to them too like all human beings. I need to also acknowledge that there are also a lot of teenagers out there that are carers to their own parents due to illness or disabilities that are doing wonderful jobs!

So although I very much look at the negative behaviours of teenagers in this book, I want to acknowledge that they do have positive qualities and can be very endearing sometimes.

> WHEN THEY ARE CUTE THEY ARE VERY, VERY CUTE BUT WHEN THEY ARE BAD THEY ARE HORRID!

This book focuses on the challenging behaviours of teenagers and it is specifically for parents that are struggling with these difficulties.

"No child comes with an instruction book" you will hear many parents and professionals say. Well this is in a sense an instruction book, although we have to bear in mind that all children are unique and what works for one child may not work for another.

These are basic guidelines for parents to adopt and adapt to suit their unique child.

It is quite tricky for professionals working with parents as they can often understandably be quite sensitive to being given advice, they can feel that it is a criticism of their parenting.

Also a Mum or Dad can come in and tell us what a 'cheeky monkey' their child is, but if a professional talks about their 'cheeky monkey' behaving badly it can feel like a criticism of their child.

In both cases it is not, it is encouragement for you to grow as a parent and ways in which therapist can help you to support the growth of your child.

If you have got this far in the parenting process, than you have done a pretty good job. You have got through the 'terrible two's,' the 'where, what and why three and four's,' the 'messy five to seven's', the 'argumentative eight to ten' years and the 'stroppy ten to twelve' years.

Congratulations! You have survived those stages and are still smiling, and still 'in love' with your child.

For the next stage on your parenting journey you need as parents to have a teenager survival kit, this book provides you with a mini survival kit. Here are six tips to begin with:

1. Look after yourself. It is important to carry on looking after yourslf when you are under stress
2. Stay calm
3. Keep talking and listening
4. Set and keep to boundaries

5. Allow teenagers to have time alone
6. Don't give in to bad behaviour

You are at your final stage before they go out into the big wide world and may eventually have kids of their own, with lessons learned that will help them with their own parenting skills and you can relax and enjoy the joys of being a Grandparent.

> "I thought teenagers were supposed to lock themselves in their rooms and never talk to their parents?
>
> I was kinda looking forward to that!"

Chapter One

Accepting that teenagers are on a different Planet!

> A school receives a telephone call. "Hello," says the principal. "My daughter won't be in school today," says the voice. "May I ask who this is?" asked the principal. "This is my mother speaking."

Pluto is the second most massive known dwarf planet in the solar system. In Roman Mythology Pluto is the God of the underworld named because it is in perpetual darkness.

Pluto is known for its odd behaviour due to its eccentric orbit around the sun. It has caused a lot of confusion for astrologists and since it was first discovered it has captivated their minds on whether this mysterious unknown force could be called a planet or if it was a remnant of a wayward comet somehow sucked off course.

To date there is still confusion amongst the gazers of the planets on this tiny but cold rock.

I am sure therefore you can see the reason that I decided to call this book 'Teenagers are from Pluto." Don't worry they will then develop into Men from Mars and Women from Venus, hopefully when they reach adulthood (See book Men are from Mars and Women are from Venus by John Grey).

If we are from Mars and Venus then where would our teenagers be from? I became an amateur astrologist and studied the role of a variety of planets.

Pluto was the one that struck a chord when thinking of the behaviours of a teenager. For the following reasons:

1. Pluto is a dwarf planet – teenagers are mini adults
2. Pluto is in perpetual darkness – it can feel like our teenagers are in a darker world than us sometimes
3. Pluto is known for its odd and eccentric behavior – teenagers are known for this type of behavior
4. It is has caused a lot of confusion for astrologists – teenagers can cause a lot of confusion for parents
5. And last but not least, Pluto is a mysterious unknown force and may be a remnant of a wayward comet somehow sucked off course – Well that says it all, aren't teenagers a mysterious unknown force, and a wayward human being sucked off course for a while?

So my mind made up this was going to be the title of my book. "Teenagers are from Pluto." For the purpose of this book I have also invented the name "Plutonian" for our teenager offspring! (Don't let them hear you call them this though, not unless you want world war three to start or a twelve hour sulking marathon).

So our first lesson is that as parents we need to accept that our teenagers are from a different planet to us, they certainly will see us as being on another planet, so it's time that we recognised that they were on one too. Therefore until they decide to join the same planet as we are on, we are going to need a survival kit to see us through these sometimes difficult times.

We will <u>never</u> understand the full complexities of teenagers, books have been written over the years, research has been carried out and just when we think we have got a handle on it society changes and so does the behaviour of the teenager, bringing about new adventures and new dangers.

Some things do not change though and in society through the years the most predominant onset of adolescence is a dramatic change in behaviour around their parents.

They start to separate from Mum and Dad and become more independent. They become increasingly aware of how others, especially their peers, see them and they desperately try to fit in.

Their peers become the most important people in their lives now and not their parents and it is with them that they make their decisions.

They will start trying on different looks and identities and they become aware of how they differ from their peers, which can result in episodes of distress and conflict with their parents.

Another thing to consider when raising plutonians are HORMONES! Teen hormones affect teenager's moods, emotions and impulses as well as their body. The mood swings that plutonians experience are caused by fluctuations in estrogen, progesterone and testosterone – the SEX hormones. These same teen hormones will affect the way they think about dating and sex. Plutonians need to be taught about 'safe sex' despite how uncomfortable that this may be for all planets – so ignore the plutonian grunts and groan's and sit them down for discussion.

They may say there is no need as they know it all, if so ask them what they know. This gives you the opportunity to correct any misconceptions and who knows you may learn something new too!

Parents can suddenly start to feel excluded from their lives, they can start to feel redundant and wonder where their precious 'little darling' as disappeared to and who is this person that has replaced them.

Martians and Venetians may start arguing about their offspring, you will be surprised how many divorces happen when children reach adolescence. Hang on in there it does end, it does come to an end. The important thing is that the Plutonians do not see this, as that feeds into their own behaviours of manipulation. (Playing one against the other).

Also, from my experience I observed that a lot of the conflict between Martians, Venetians and their visiting

Plutonian is when parents try to stop the Plutonian from making the same mistakes as they did. Martians and Venetians are very good at seeing into the future and when they see negative outcomes for the future that their plutonian has planned, they may try to stop them from pursuing their future plan. Don't!

The first thing that we have to do is to remember that they are not the same as us; they have not gone through the same experiences so they do not have the same knowledge. We have to remember that we gained that knowledge experimentally and we have to allow our teenagers to do the same within reason.

There is absolutely no point in trying to stop them from making the same mistakes as we did, because they will do it anyway and we will be too exhausted trying to prevent them from making those mistakes that we will have no energy left to pick up the pieces of their pain when they fall flat on their face!

> A Plutonian is a person that can never remember to walk the dog but never forgets their friend's phone number!

Think about when they were two or three years old and you were trying to teach them how to ride their bike without their stabilisers on.

Did you hold on to the back bar for dear life, running along behind them until they were eight?

OR

Did you let go and just stand back ready with a sticky plaster in your hand, to help them and nurture them if they fell off?

I have no doubt that every parent reading this book will say the second one.

Well, that is what you need to do as a parent of a teenager, unless you feel that they are at risk of putting themselves in serious danger of course.

You need to stand back and let them go, let them ride their world without stabilisers. Let them fall and be there with the 'sticky plaster' – a soothing hand when they do. For short moments you will have your little boy or girl back needing their mummy and daddy and feel needed again.

The hardest part for parents is the letting go, letting their babies fly, losing in a sense a little control.

If you can manage to do this then like baby chicks they will return to the nest, they will be more communicative and have more respect for you. If you cannot, then the battles will be harder and you will have little or no information at all of their lives. They will be defensive and wary of you and if they feel that you are trying to control their lives then they will cut you out of it completely.

> Plutonian's have a pact amongst them that says "Keep out Martians and Venetians!"

It is about learning to use reverse psychology and unleashing the control to gain their trust to make it easier for them to communicate with you, therefore you will have more information about what they are doing, and feel more in control.

A plutonian may want to experience the ways of the Martians and Venetians, they may want to try sex, cars and drink, if you have good communications with them then you will be able to ensure that they do all of these things in a safe way!

Like Martians and Venetians, a plutonian wants and needs independence, but like children they are still in the business of testing boundaries. Sometimes they are not happy just to test the boundaries; they will jump up and down and stamp on them!

So, you may have brought this book because you now have a plutonian in the house! Good luck!

We hope that this instruction book helps you to adapt your parenting style, as it will need to change. Too many parents will try to change the plutonian, rather than their parenting style and that is where the battle begins.

A plutonian will eventually change him or herself, when s/he is ready to be a Martian or a Venetian. However you can change you, which will help you to manage this plutonian invasion of your home better.

These are some of the changes you might wish to make:

    A. Know what your bottom line is and stick to it
    B. Teach your child to problem solve
    C. Now become the teacher, coach and limit setter.
    D. Aim for small victories

E. Work on one behavour at a time, anymore and you become a nag and they stop listening
F. Avoid giving away your power
G. Establish clear boundaries
H. Utilize assertive and effective communication
I. In mild situations maintain humor and show empathy
J. Ignore your child's shrugs, raised eyes and bored looks if s/he's generally behaving the way you would like him/her to
K. Check your understanding
L. Give your child descriptive praise when s/he communicates in a positive way

Last but by no means least spend time with you Plutonian.

Make yourself available to talk when s/he expresses interest in doing so. As inconvenient as it might feel, don't see yourself as just the taxi driver, offer to give your Plutonian a lift and then use the time in the car to chat. Sometimes sitting side by side can offer a more comfortable venue for conversation. Stay involved as much as s/he allows in his/her everyday life.

Keep at the forefront of your mind that you are not alone, parents are dealing with teenagers all over the world at the same time as you are. It is challenging, worrying and sometimes a distressing time. While plutonians are pushing against the system in their search for independence, we need to hang on to the parachute until we hit the ground.

You have to learn the rules of the game and then you have to play it better than your plutonian!

> Teenager to his fellow plutonian: "Every time that I say that I am bored, my mom hears "I want to do chores!"

Chapter Two

Are both parents beating from the same drum?!

> Teenager to his family: "Do not touch **MY** I phone! It is not an **'US'** phone, it is not a **'WE'** phone, it is not an **'OUR'** phone. It is an **'I'** Phone!"

The most important thing when raising children and in particular teenagers is that 'mum' and 'dad' are beating from the same drum.

The minute that their teenage offspring perceive that they are not, is the minute that they start playing one parent off against the other. This applies to both being a single parent or joint parents.

Both parents of a plutonian will have been raised in separate households; therefore they have brought to the relationship diverse values and experiences around parenting. For example Mum, may have had quite laid back parents whereas Dad may have had quite strict parenting.

Mum therefore might think ten o'clock is a fair time for their fourteen year old to come in at night and Dad may think that this is far too late. Or parents may wish to raise their children the opposite to how they were raised.

This causes massive problems between couples when raising children and can create lots of rows. So it is extremely important for parents to iron their differing ideas of parenting out before communications begin with their offspring.

Rowing about boundaries and behavioural acceptances or non acceptances in front of the child is the worst thing that you can do, and will result in 'game playing' by the plutonian.

This is extremely important, so find some time to sit down to have that discussion about boundaries and reach a compromise. Why not go out to that restaurant for a meal that you have never got around to doing and have the discussion there. Having time for you is really important for parents, although the plutonian may think that s/he is the centre of the world right now, don't make him/her the centre of your world. Have that discussion then have fun! Remember life before you became parents to a plutonian.

If you look at the following triangle in the bottom two corners are the parents and at the top are the children.

If both parents are working together then they have a solid foundation to hold up the triangle (the children being at the top).

CHILDREN

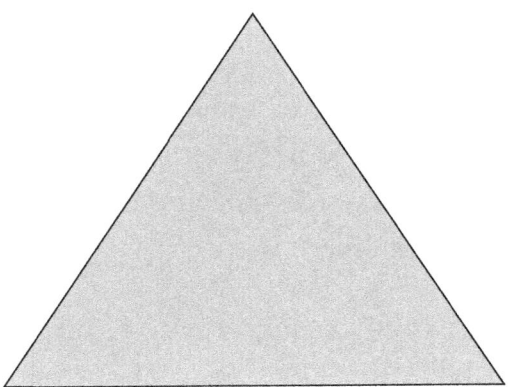

MUM   **DAD**

However if they do not have those solid foundations one of two things can happen:

1. A parent and a child are at the bottom and one parent is at the top, this is when one parent is colluding with the child against the other parent. The child's behavior will become predominantly worse towards <u>both</u> parents.

2. The parents are in conflict causing the top to collapse and the battle with your teenage child will get worse.

Once that you have sat together and ironed out any differences that you have in your parenting styles and worked through what is acceptable to you as parents and what is not and made compromises that will help you to find a middle ground, then you can sit down and set some ground rules for your teenage offspring.

This may need to be looked at several times over the years as new problems arise. What you need to do as a couple is to think about what behaviours are not acceptable to you. Then together set some ground rules.

I think that it is always helpful if you write down your ground rules, and after discussing them with your teenager together, putting a copy up in your home so there can be no mistaking what you have decided.

Note that I said 'together.' Where possible, all meetings, boundary, rules and consequence setting needs to be done together with the teenager. You need to show a united front.

The plutonian may make all attempts to avoid this discussion, after all what do you know you are just restrictive planets and why should they listen to you. Here is some guidance, for those discussions:

- ✓ Remove distractions. When you really want to talk with your plutonian, stop all distractions and outside stimuli
- ✓ Be clear and keep your tone neutral
- ✓ Don't use words that shut down the conversation
- ✓ Set the stage for a more open discussion
- ✓ Don't expect a long conversation

Another point that I think is important to mention is that as parents you do not play 'good cop, bad cop' – for one it is not fair on the parent always having to play the 'bad cop.' Secondly, that allows the plutonian to try to manipulate the parent who is the 'good cop'.

When setting ground rules, do not bombard your plutonian with a list of 'do's' and 'don'ts', better to get five rules accepted and obeyed than twenty ignored.

A Plutonian is unable to internalise too much information all at once, and let's face it they are receiving data from school, college and home and of course they need to remember all the activities in their social diary too. God forbid if they let a fellow plutonian down!

Once these are set and your plutonian has internalised them and is meeting your wishes you can then add more at a later day. Here is an example of ground some ground rules and how to present them:

Ground Rules for a peaceful home

15th August 1995

1. Please do not smoke in the house. Please use bench in back garden.
2. Please be in for nine p.m. on a week night and ten p.m at weekends.
3. It would be helpful if you kept your own room tidy, and tidied up after you around the house i.e. put plates away, wash your own cups etc. Also please can you sort out your own washing?
4. Can you only play your loud music when we are out of the house, at times when we are in, it needs to be at an acceptable decibel to enable us to enjoy our programmes on the television.
5. I'd like a family meeting on the last Friday of every month to discuss how these new plans are working out and to air any issues that have arisen from them.

Thank you for your support!

With all ground rules they are no good without consequences. When there are not any consequences to someone's poor behaviour than change is unlikely to occur.

Although, as a couple you need to discuss consequences, I would advise that initially no consequences are discussed at this point, as you are asking your plutonian to meet you half way.

If you put in consequences at this stage s/he may become defensive and rebel. After all s/he is in the final stage before adulthood and should be given the opportunity to respond in an adult way.

Once the ground rules are agreed between you both then the first thing to do is arrange a time when you can all sit down as a family and put your request to the plutonian, giving him/her a copy of these rules.

S/he may stomp his/her feet but make it clear that these are your rules and you expect him/her to adhere to them.

Arrange another family meeting to discuss progress. While you are having difficulties with your plutonian I would recommend that you have regular family meetings.

Every family is different but I would suggest weekly or fortnightly meetings at first and then monthly when things are more settled.

At the first family meeting discussion after you have set the ground rules, it is best that initially the communications be around the new ground rules and how s/he is managing to maintain them.

If there are any that s/he is not maintaining, ask how you can support him/her in maintaining them. i.e. are there any difficulties in maintaining them.

Ground rules are <u>not</u> to be changed but at this point compromises can be made i.e. washing is difficult due to him/her not knowing how to use the washing machine, this is manageable because you can teach him/her.

While your plutonian is open to change, compromise, and agreement to your ground rules. 'Consequences' may not be needed.

In the event that s/he rebels and ignores any of your ground rules remind him/her that wherever s/he lives there will be 'rules' and much more tougher ones than the ones that you are imposing.

If s/he continues to ignore your requests, then this is the time to set those consequences that you discussed, thinking of my ground rules the consequences may be:

1. If s/he does not respect our home then he will need to go further away to have a cigarette i.e. down the street.

2. If s/he does not pick up his pots and put them in the dishwasher then he will need to go to the local café for

his meals, as there is a waitress service there that will be quite happy to pick up after him.

3. If s/he does not take some responsibility for their washing then there is a launderette down the road, they will need to do their washing there at their own expense.

4. If the loud music continues at unreasonable times then as this is our home and everything in it belongs to us, the hi fi system will be put in the loft until such time as it can be used reasonably.

The most important thing to remember about consequences is that you have to follow them through, so do not set consequences that you cannot follow through as this will weaken your position and make sure that you are both willing to follow them through. If one partner is reluctant then the battle will be harder for you.

Some more guidance to consider:

- Remember to tie privileges to good behaviour
- Avoid repetition
- Enforce consequences
- Have a plan
- Praise good behaviour

- Teach problem solving
- Focus on one behaviour
- Pick your battles

I know that you may be keen to put this into action now, please hold fire until you read the rest of this book as there are other tools that you may need to put in place first.

Chapter Three

There is no such thing as the 'perfect parent'

> Two teenagers are talking to each other. One says,
>
> "I'm really worried. My dad works twelve hours a day to give me a nice home and good food. My mom spends the whole day cleaning and cooking for me. I'm worried sick!"
>
> The other kid says, "What have you got to worry about? Sounds to me like you've got it made!"
>
> The first kid says, "What if they try to escape?"

One of the biggest mistakes parents of teenagers make is a need to be a 'perfect parent' or a need to be liked by their teenage offspring.

You will not succeed at either.

We are not 'perfect human beings' let alone 'perfect parents' and to try to be so is an unachievable goal and will set you up for continuous failures.

Your teenager from Pluto will want you to be perfect, but his perception of a perfect parent is someone who lets him/her do whatever s/he wants. And of course, everyone else's parent will be better than you!

BE AWARE that a plutonian has a favourite phrase. It has been coming out of their mouths for centuries and it is:

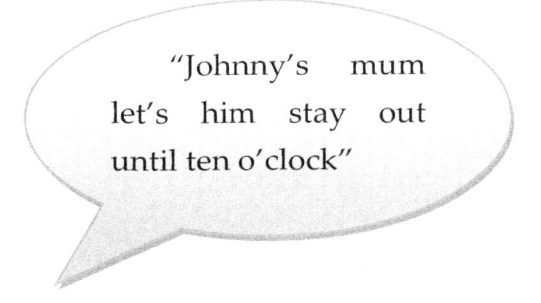

> "Johnny's mum let's him stay out until ten o'clock"

Or whatever s/he is wanting you to let him/her do

<u>**Don't believe them**</u>. You can guarantee Johnny is probably saying the same thing to his mum!

One of the things that a plutonian will do regularly is tell 'little white lies' and some will tell whoppers!

If s/he's telling the truth, that Johnny's mum let's him stay out until ten o'clock, then so be it, Johnny's mum has a different parenting style than you and that's okay. Stick to your parenting style because this is your child.

From my experience there are four things that prevent us from practising tough love with our teenage offspring and they are:

1. Our overwhelming love for them
2. A need for us to be liked/loved and needed
3. Other people's perceptions of our parenting
4. Guilt

So it may be helpful to look at those now:

Our overwhelming love for them:

Firstly, love is not about acceptance of bad behaviour towards us, and secondly to set boundaries in a relationship is done out of love for them and for ourselves. They are to protect them and to prepare them for their independence.

If we did not love them, then we would not care what they did or how they fared in the future.

So it is out of overwhelming love that we practice tough love!

Our need for us to be liked or loved and needed:

All of us as human beings, (and despite what our teenagers think, <u>**we are human beings)**</u><u>,</u> have a need to be liked or loved and particularly by our children.

Get real, they will hate you and they will tell you every day how much they hate you, particularly if they are not getting their own way, and particularly above all, if they know that it hurts you.

But, just as we love our children, there are times when we do not like them very much. It is the same the opposite way round. Deep down they love you, they just don't like the way you are behaving towards them at the moment and they are ignorant to your genuine motives.

Remember that there is a very fine line between love and hate. You can't hate someone that you don't love, so take it as a compliment. If your plutonian hates you then you can be sure that s/he loves you.

Other people's perceptions of you as a parent:

A plutonian is notorious for going out and telling their friends what a 'wicked parent' they have. They do it for sympathy and sometimes attention. A Plutonian can be very attention seeking.

If we worry about what their friends or their friend's parents will say, then this will be a barrier to tough love, and they will play on that.

I was terrible if it came to disciplining my children in company. I wouldn't do it because I did not want to be seen as a bad parent. My children picked up on this.

> A Plutonian has very good observation skills and their favourite pastime is to observe the behaviours of Martians and Venetians.

My children observing that they never got told off when other people were around subsequently would play up when we were in company.

The truth of the matter is my fellow Venetians probably said behind my back, "She lets her children get away with too much," writing me off as a bad parent anyway.

So don't fall for that one. If they behave badly in public then they should be disciplined in public, showing everyone what a 'good and responsible parent' that you are.

Besides they will hate being told off in public more than you do telling them off in public. So their behaviour will subsequently change in public, after one telling off in public, you watch.

Oh yes without a doubt they will chastise you for embarrassing them, but you can of course remind them that they may want to consider that they may have embarrassed themselves.

And last but not least guilt:

One of the feelings that most parents carry around with them is:

GUILT

- ✓ We feel guilty for working and leaving our children in day care.
- ✓ We feel guilty for not working and not giving our children enough material things.
- ✓ We feel guilty for not always being able to be emotionally there for them.
- ✓ We feel guilty for not always having the time for them.
- ✓ We feel guilty for not taking them to all the places that we would have liked to take them.
- ✓ We feel guilty for our marriage breakdown, and taking a parent away from them.
- ✓ We feel guilty for disciplining them.

And so on and so on.

As hard as it is these feelings have to be acknowledged, 'GUILT is a requisition of the job' they are normal feelings, but then they need to be put aside. They should not influence your parenting.

So pop that 'guilt' feeling in the bin because you have done your very best as a parent with the resources that you had at the time and that is all any child can ask for.

Don't let your plutonian visitor know that you feel 'Guilt'; they love that feeling and will go to all lengths to reinforce it.

To be swallowed up by these feelings of guilt will only create more problems for you in the long run because:

1. You will be too soft with your children.
2. They will hinder your attempts at tough love
3. They will instigate a need for you to over compensate with your children.

A plutonian will feed off our guilt as they are quite astute. They have been living with you for a lot of years, and they soon pick up what you feel guilty about and will play on that.

Also it is worth mentioning that a plutonian will, without a doubt listen in on your conversations, they have a storage system and they will store information that they can use against you at a later date. So be warned!

There is no such thing as a perfect parent just as there is no such thing as a perfect child.

When that guilt sneaks up on you, have a mantra ready that you can repeat to yourself in your head that will reinforce your 'good parenting', I will share mine with you:

"Look on the bright side they could have been born to Fred and Rose West if they had they would be under the patio by now!"

"As a parent I did my best!"

Stick with doing all that you can, and remind yourself that you are doing what you think is the best at that moment in time.

- ➢ **Stay Positive** – things can change, don't assume the worst of your plutonian or s/he will believe that too. Try to be a positive voice in their lives.
- ➢ **Like them** – try to separate the behaviour from the person. Remind yourself of all their good qualities. Your plutonian may be behaving badly but that doesn't make them a bad person.
- ➢ **Be reassuring** – plutonian's are scared by all their mixed up feelings right now and all the responsibilities that they feel that they have. They need your reassurance that they are not going mad.
- ➢ **Be there** – They will still need to talk but at their own pace and in their own time. Listen to them without interruption and don't tell them what to do, they don't want advice they just want to be heard.
- ➢ **Be patient** – plutonians are trying to find the right balance of behaviours and independence, they will swing too far in the opposite direction, but in time they will swing back to the right balance and become more settled.

- **Be loving** – Your plutonian may push you away, but they still need your love, so no matter how hard they push remind them that you love them.
- **Be empathic** – Your plutonian may act as though they are indestructible, but they are usually very fragile – handle with care.
- **Forgive and forget** – Don't hold grudges, your plutonian will be holding enough for all of you. Teach him/her how to move forward by demonstrating healthy behaviours they will learn to mirror this.
- **Be hopeful** – Remember this is only a phase, just like all the other phases they have gone through. They will come back and develop a meaningful relationship with you that will last for years.

Teenagers are even harder to handle than toddlers as they stay up later which means that you have to deal with them for longer. Young children understand that they are not yet adults, teenagers have no such ability.

Chapter Four

Tough Love – Be Consistent with firm boundaries

> A father was trying to teach his young son the evils of alcohol.
>
> He put one worm in a glass of water and another worm in a glass of whiskey. The worm in the water lived, while the one in the whiskey curled up and died.
>
> "All right, son," asked the father, "what does that show you?"
>
> "Well, Dad, it shows that if you drink alcohol, you will not have worms."

You are dealing with an unusual species when dealing with a plutonian. Look at some of their odd behaviours:

S/he will not turn their head when you call their name.

They can lie on the sofa for hours on end without moving, and they do not bother to take their boots off.

Some may go days, even weeks without having a wash, or clean their teeth and if you ask them to change their bed sheets, then that will be a cardinal sin!

They roam about the streets and may not return until the middle of the night if you let them, with no thought for anyone else.

They will think that they have nine lives and may put themselves in risky situations due to this belief.

They will not share your taste in music or television programmes and no matter what you do for them it is never enough!

They will expect you to wait on them hand and foot and solve all their problems for them.

They will come and go as they please and will treat your home like a hotel.

They will constantly protest that they are bored and expect you to fix that for them and the super glue to fix their boredom is usually found in your purse or wallet! Designer gear is their fix – they compete with each other on who has got the latest in designer gear.

They may spend hours and hours on the computer and delete their history so that you are unable to see what they have been doing.

Therefore I cannot stress enough the importance of consistent and firm boundaries being in place for plutonians.

You have heard the saying "Give him an inch and he will take a yard" - This cannot be more significant than when dealing with this species.

First of all let's clarify what a boundary is:

> A boundary is a limit on what is reasonable
>
> They help to clarify what are acceptable and unacceptable behaviours from others
>
> Effective boundaries are the foundation of all healthy relationships; they help to develop trust, stability and respect
>
> Setting boundaries asserts the needs or rights of families so that they feel secure and respected

Now let's explore the key areas for both parents to look at when setting boundaries:

YOUR TIME: Time is an important personal asset. Does your teenager make unreasonable demands on your time? Do they expect you to change your plans?

YOUR EMOTIONS: Your emotions are where your love and caring comes from. They should be well protected. Does your teenager say or do hurtful things (often unintentional)? Been thoughtless? Does he hook into your emotions and manipulate this?

YOUR ENERGY: Your energy comes from your inner peace, your activities, your personal time etc. Does your teenager invade your privacy, make unreasonable demands? This means that you are unable to function effectively.

YOUR SAFETY: Do you feel threatened? Do you feel at risk?

YOUR HOME AND PROPERTY: Does your teenager make threats against your possessions? Do they steal from you? Do they treat your house like a hotel?

We will be exploring some of those things in this book but for now, ask yourself this question:

Have you been sending mixed messages for years about what is acceptable and what isn't, what you will tolerate and what you won't?

If so, you may have perfected the boy-who-cried-wolf syndrome by not establishing and sticking with firm boundaries and consequences. Therefore if you are going to make changes you need to be able to stick to them through rain or shine.

Your plutonian needs to know that you are serious, and that you mean business!

> A teenager is a boy who can sleep until noon on any Saturday when he suspects the lawn needs mowing!

Be warned that a Plutonian does not like boundaries.

They kick and stomp in rebellion or sulk and sometimes they can conjure up false tears. Don't fall for it; they are usually what we call crocodile tears and they have learned from an early age that these get there needs met. To continue to respond or react to this behaviour will only encourage them to continue with this unhealthy performance when they enter adulthood.

And Martians (Dad's) don't fall for the fluttering of the eyelashes either. A female plutonian will have also learned from an early age that to flutter their eyelashes at Martians can often get them their needs met. Martians are suckers for this. If you respond or react then you are making it more difficult for the Martian that she marries!

Remember you are the parent, you are not their friend, and you are there to give them boundaries that they need to become a functional responsible adult. They may hate you right now but it is your jobs to raise a responsible adult not nurture bad habits in your teenage child.

> Teenagers are like a Chinese buffet
>
> Lots of sweet and sour and as rational as the inside of a fortune cookie!

Remember, if you are really struggling with being 'the bad guy' right now, then you can always get yourself a dog, at least someone in the house will be happy to see you, right now.

When setting boundaries please take note of the following:

   I.   We need to have a clearly defined action plan before confronting our teenager
  II.   We need to establish consequences and stick with them
 III.   We need to present a unified front if in a relationship
  IV.   We must not get involved in a debate or discussion
   V.   We need to encourage our teenager to figure things out for themselves
  VI.   We need to ask ourselves "Who am I outside of this issue/teenager?
 VII.   We must be willing to shift the focus off the life of our teenager, and onto our own.

Hopefully the tools in this book will help you to do the above.

Remember that sometimes they may think you are always on their back, what they don't realise just yet is that you are the only one that has their back!

One additional point when enforcing rules, boundaries and consequences, and that is every child is unique with a unique set of problems, and what works with one child is not necessarily going to work with another.

So just when you think you have it all 'in the bag' after the first one, you have to relearn again for the next.

NO PLUTONIAN IS THE SAME

I had three children and the consequence of grounding for example worked very differently for all three.

Child number One: Grounding was not an issue to him, because he'd walk out anyway either through the door if I was not looking or out the window if I was.

Child number Two: Would hate being grounded and unable to cope with one day of being unable to socialise with her friends so would tidy up, be on her best behaviour to ensure that I did not prolong her grounding period.

Child number Three: Would not be bothered if she was grounded, it had no effect on her at all if she was not allowed to socialise with her friends for a week or a month.

When your plutonian crosses the line and if you really think that it is about time for him/her to pay some consequence to their actions, instead of giving the usual consequences such as grounding, confiscating technology or phones which will instigate him/her to turn against you. Why not try something different?

Instead teach your plutonian a lesson where they will learn certain values; make him/her help you with the household chores or take you plutonian for a visit to an orphanage and help out which will help your plutonian to realise how lucky s/he is to have you, and hopefully encourage more responsible behaviours. Give it a try, devise a list with your partner in crime and come up with original ideas for consequences. You could even have a 'consequence bag' with them in and when they need to be administered ask your plutonian to dip into the 'lucky dip' to see what consequence s/he has to do.

> **TEENAGERS**
> tired of being
> harassed by
> your parents?
>
> **ACT NOW!**
> Move out, Get a job,
> & Pay your own way,
>
> **QUICK!**
> while you still
> know everything!

Families vary enormously in terms of the amount of time they spend together, whether or not they eat together, take part in activities together, discuss issues routinely, and when there are crises.

Generally families function better when they communicate regularly with each other. That is why I always recommend and encourage family members to meet together regularly as a group each week.

Define a regular time each week when it is most convenient to devote 30 minutes to a family meeting where you can discuss relevant issues. As well as keeping communications alive, it can prepare your plutonian for work where s/he may have to attend meetings. Make it fun but structured; to help with this process you could do the following:

Elect a secretary to organise the family meetings. Duties may include:

Collecting items for discussion
Prompting attendance by household members
Keeping notes on items discussed

Elect a chairperson to structure the discussions during the family meeting. Duties may include:

Ensuring that meetings begin and end on time
Prompting people to keep discussions to the point
Ensuring every person has his/her say and feel able to express themselves freely
Ensuring that people behave appropriately

Some plutonian's like a family meeting, but they won't necessarily admit to it, put on chocolate biscuits and s/he will be the first there!

Another thing you may want to do at family meetings is to get an important message across to your plutonian.

A plutonian does not understand or is able to internalise long winded conversations. They call it 'nagging' and very easily nod off, when someone starts nagging.

Once the ground rules have been put in place and family life is running a little smoother, you can introduce quotes into that time as a way of getting a message across.

By that I mean that anyone at anytime can bring a card with a quote written on it. They can then pass it to the person they want to 'get the message' and ask them for their interpretation. The whole family can then contribute their interpretation.

For example:

Johnny the plutonian is participating in risky behaviour that may affect his future. So to get that message across without nagging, I might take the following quote along:

> **"The house that you build today, may have to be the one you live in tomorrow, so build wisely"**

Hopefully, Johnny or the family will interpret that and Johnny will get the message.

Quotes and metaphors can be found on the internet, and I have included some at the end of some of the chapters in this book.

This can be far more powerful than long winded conversations about his/her behaviour, less is more so to speak, and can also be fun.

Holding on to anger is like holding on to a hot coal, the only one to get burnt will be you, and did you know that every minute that you are angry you lose sixty seconds of happiness!

Chapter Five

You will never be your child's best friend

> A teacher said to his students: "If there are any idiots in the room, will they please stand up"
>
> After a long silence, one freshman rose to his feet.
>
> "Now then mister, why do you consider yourself an idiot?" enquired the teacher with a sneer.
>
> "Well, actually I don't," said the student, "but I hate to see you standing up there all by yourself."

I meet a lot of parents who have this dream that when their children become teenagers, they can be mates, best friends even. I am not sure that this is always possible. One would need to have a very grown up teenager who is able to separate the two relationships from each other to enable this to work, and in my experience teenagers are not 'grown up', they are 'growing up.'

To be your teenagers best friend creates inconsistency in your relationship because one minute you are doing what best friends do, going out together, sharing secrets, clothes and make up and the next you are telling him/her what time to be in at night. Teenagers in particular need consistency.

It is a healthy household when children have their own friends and parents have their own friends. You can't be their friend and their parent/teacher, the boundaries become too blurred.

So be aware when thinking of making a plutonian your best friend, you both have to be able to keep the two relationships separate. Is that possible with your plutonian?

One of our roles as parents and not friends is to teach our teenagers to follow directions, and this is one of the most challenging tasks that we have as parents.

A plutonian only knows one direction and that is the way to his or her hang out place, so to instil directions into their memories becomes a tiring task!

It becomes frustrating for the whole family when parents have to repeatedly give their plutonian the same directions over and over again.

"Pick your clothes up"

"Put your plates away"

"Pick your clothes up"

"Make your bed"

"Put your plates away"

Do you ever get sick of hearing your own voice or that of your partners saying the same thing over and over again?

This need's to change and this is how you can change.

Be prepared to enforce. Parents should avoid giving their teenagers a direction unless they are prepared to enforce it. If parents do not enforce their directions, then teenagers learn that their parents don't mean what they say.

Get their attention. Parents should always get their teenager's attention before giving a direction. Parents should avoid yelling directions from another room.

Don't ask questions. Parents should avoid phrasing directions as questions (for example, don't say "Johnny, would you like to pick up your shoes now?" You are giving them the option to say "No!"

Don't be vague. Parents should avoid giving vague directions such as "Be good," or "Be careful." There may be significant differences between how the parent and teenager interpret vague directions such as "being good." Parents should make their directions clear and specific.

Tell them what to do. Parents should try to give directions that tell teenagers what to do instead of what not to do. For example, it is better to say, "Be in at ten o'clock," than "be in no later than ten o'clock."

Praise them. Parents should praise their teenager as soon as they have begun to follow the direction. Parents don't need to wait until the task is completed to offer praise.

Show appreciation. When the task is complete, parents should let their teenager know that they appreciate their compliance.

Give time limit. If the teenager does not start to follow a direction within ten seconds to two minutes, parents should put in a consequence.

Don't repeat warnings. Parents should avoid giving their teenagers repeated warnings. They need to learn to follow directions after one or no warning just as easily as they can learn to follow directions after five or six warnings.

Repeat the direction. After the consequence is complete, parents should repeat the direction to their teenager. If they do not start to follow the direction, a consequence should be used again. This process should be repeated until the teenager complies with the direction.

Acknowledging their positive activities and behaviour:

It is also important for teenagers to view their parents as people who offer a lot of positive attention. The following suggestions can help you to improve in this area.

Catch them being good. To be able to acknowledge a teenagers positive behaviour, it is important that parents monitor their teenager's activities frequently. This will give parents a chance to observe more of their teenager's appropriate behaviours. Try to listen to what they say no matter how busy you are, they may be telling you that they helped a lady cross the road today. If not you may have lost an opportunity to give them praise.

Don't wait for a special occasion. Parents should offer their teenager a lot of praise when they are behaving "ok." Parents should not wait until their teenager does something extraordinary to offer praise.

Be specific. When parents praise their teenager, it is often a good idea to tell them exactly why they are being praised. For example, "You did a great job of not interrupting me while I was speaking on the telephone. Thanks."

Provide physical attention. In addition to verbal praise, parents should offer a lot of physical attention. For example, hugs, smiles, kisses, pats on the back, or winks. They are never too big for a hug, no matter how much they might say differently.

Give immediate feedback. It is important to give teenagers positive feedback immediately. Parents shouldn't wait until sometime after the good behaviour occurs to offer the praise.

Avoid backhanded compliments. It is important to avoid using backhanded compliments. For example, it is not a good idea to say something like "That's good; why can't you do that more often?"

Use third-handed compliments. Third-handed compliments can be very effective. Third-handed compliments occur when one person tells another person about a teenager's good behaviour in the teenager's presence. For example, when one parent comes home from work, the other parent talks about the teenager's good behaviour that occurred that day.

Plan parent-teenager activities. The use of a parent-teenager activity can still be used to reward their good behaviour. For example: going to the park or ice skating or having a video night. The use of parent-teenage activities is often preferable to the use of material rewards.

So if this is our role as parents, how can we possibly be their best friends too?

We cannot be everything to our children and for any parent who wishes their children to be their best friend at this age, I would question their emotional needs, rather than the child's.

Having said all that a friendly house is a peaceful home, so there is no harm in being friendly and having fun with your teenager.

It is okay to 'hang out' with them occasionally, that can make you a better parent, get in touch with the 'child' within you, use your imagination and rekindle your creativity so that it is fun for your children to hang out with you.

They need to be able to trust you, and be able to talk to you and they need to hear shared confidences with you too. It helps them to feel like a 'grown up' – this does not mean being their best friend, just two adults sharing.

Almost every kid wonders about his or her parent's teenage years. Were they awkward, or as horny or rebellious? They want to know how they can relate to their parents. The better and more interesting your stories are the more they can relate to you. Don't tell them bad stories and be a bad influence in a colluding kind of way. Turn a bad story into a joke and an encouraging life lesson for them. It will encourage them to talk to you more.

This is communication rather than trying to be your teen's best friend.

> Happiness leads to a good self esteem!

Chapter Six

Caring for teenagers, rather than rescuing

> Teenage Girl to her friend: "I'm never having kids. I hear they take nine months to download."

One of the difficulties that parents struggle with, in my experience, and one of the things that is often disagreed about in many a household as parents is how much do you actually do for your teenagers, particularly the practical stuff.

If you do too much then you may be mollycoddling them, and if you don't do enough then you may be neglecting them.

The important thing to remember is that we are preparing our teenagers for adulthood, when they will have to do most things for themselves, so it is about finding the right balance.

A good measure is to listen to your own body; if your teenager is wearing you out then you are doing too much, so it may be about doing less.

If you are helping the plutonian, or caring for the plutonian, then that is a good balance, however if you are enabling or rescuing your plutonian then that is not benefiting the plutonian or you.

The next few pages will explain the difference so that you can support your plutonian in a healthy way:

We will look at:

- ✓ The difference between enabling and helping
- ✓ What behaviours constitutes enabling
- ✓ Your own enabling behaviours and help to facilitate change in those behaviours

HELPING is doing something for someone that he is not capable of doing for himself.

ENABLING is doing for someone what s/he could and should be doing for himself.

So are you 'doing' for the plutonian something that s/he is capable of doing for him/herself. If so then you are not preparing your plutonian for life. You are not teaching the plutonian life skills. This will make things difficult for him/her and others in the future.

We need to prepare our children to fly, they will always come back to the nest, even if it only for the occasional Sunday lunch, but they need to be able to stand on their own two feet for when we are no longer around.

Enabling your plutonian also creates an atmosphere in which your plutonian can comfortably continue their unacceptable behaviour!

ENABLING IS:

- ◆ When we continue to allow unacceptable behaviour,
- ◆ When we are setting up a pattern with our children that will be hard to change
- ◆ When we've been repeating the same patterns for years.

WHY DO WE ENABLE:

We enable when............

- We confuse 'helping' with 'enabling'
- When we fear for our safety
- When we irrationally fear for their safety
- When we are worried about consequences
- When we feel guilty about things we did or didn't do when they were younger
- When it is all we know how to do (habit)
- It feels easier than change
- Not knowing how to stop

THE CONSEQUENCES OF ENABLING:

When we continue this behaviour our teenage children will continue to deny that they have any problems, since most of them are being 'solved' by the people around them.

It will be hard for our teenage children to develop tools for coping with their lot in life.

Our teenage children will learn to expect us to deal with all their problems., sometimes for all of our lives.

We will be consistently worn out and unable to move forward with our own lives.

When we enable it is all about our teenager and not about **us** and our needs and goals.

The last point is an important one because as a therapist I have seen a fair few Venetians enable their plutonians, to the point that either they never leave home or when they do, the Venetian suffers with 'empty nest syndrome.' This can then lead to depression. It is important that you have your own life and if you are a couple, time for each other.

So from this information do you think you are enabling your child or helping?

If you are enabling then bear in mind that it is only when your plutonian is forced to solve their own problems, or face the consequences of their own actions and choices that it will finally sink in the following:

1. How deep their own patterns of dependency are on you,

2. How strong their avoidance of doing things for them self has become.

It is only then when they will change. They will not change while you are doing everything for them!

Another tool that I found to be extremely helpful when dealing with teenagers (and useful in a lot of other areas of my life) is 'the Drama/Winners Triangle.' This is from a model of therapy called Transactional Analysis which was founded by Eric Berne.

I will try to explain this to you in relation to teenage behaviour.

First we will look at the 'Drama Triangle:'

THE DRAMA TRIANGLE

PERSECUTOR

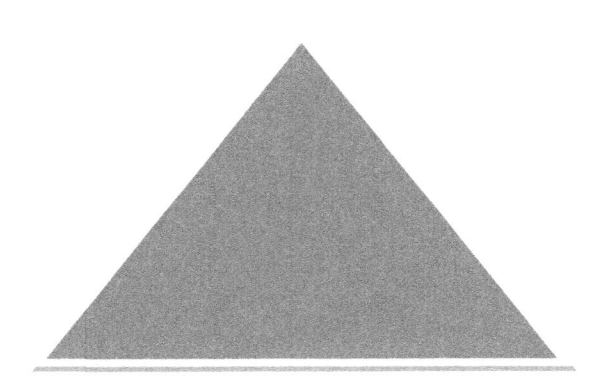

RESCUER   VICTIM

The drama triangle is the <u>unhealthy</u> triangle.

When our teenagers come to us with problems they are often in the 'victim' position and we can as parents automatically go into rescuing.

We rescue our children for lots of different reasons.

For example:

The payoff:- For a reward and that reward could be future good behaviour, a bit of peace and quiet or to be liked by them.

To get rid of:- To sort out their problem so that they won't come back to us with the same issue, to allow us to get on with our own life/day/jobs, so they don't take up too much of our time/energy. Or, to get rid of our own guilt for what we have or haven't done for them in the past.

To feel needed:- Some of us have a need to be needed and if we don't can feel lonely.

To help us:- To avoid what is going on in our own lives and the uncomfortable thoughts and feelings associated with this, or to get a bit of peace and quiet.

When we rescue our teenage children we often do not get any of the above needs met.

A plutonian will want recuing all the time, they love to play the 'victim' and a constant gripe with them is how unfair life is.

"Poor little old me" is there favourite game.

Don't fall for it!

It is there way of getting you to feel sorry for them so that they get what they want.

It is there way of reinforcing your 'guilt' feelings again so that they get what they want!

When we rescue our children, we may end up feeling resentful and angry and then we may move to the 'persecutory' position, a row may erupt and we could ourselves then become the 'victim'.

As you can see on the 'Drama Triangle,' there is potential for a 'shift' in positions.

Take five minutes to examine some of these motives:

Does it really facilitate a change in your teenager's behaviour?

Does it really get you peace and quiet, if so how long for?

Does it really get you liked; are they going out and telling their friends what a great Mom or Dad they have?

> Does it really stop them from coming back to you with the same issue?
>
> Does it really free you of time and energy?
>
> Does it eliminate your guilt feelings, if so how long for?

Let's look at an example of rescuing

> For the third day this week your child is moaning because it is raining and they have to get the bus to school or work and they will get their new trainers wet.
>
> You have been on nights and are exhausted. You do your usual rant about how in your day, you had to walk five miles to school in all weathers.
>
> Your sulky teenager stomps about the house, moaning and groaning, threatening not to go, saying that Johnny's parents take him to school every day, letting you know what a crap parent that you are, and maybe even threatening to run away from home or participate in some other dangerous activity or behaviour.
>
> For one or more of the reasons listed above you give in and take your child to work or school.
>
> Two days later the same behaviours by you and your teenager repeat themselves.

How do you feel?

When we rescue our children under the illusion that it will make things easier for us and then it doesn't, and two days later they are telling us what a bad parent we are, or they want rescuing again, or indeed the drama begins again, we feel resentful and move to the **'persecutor'** position.

We may even move to the **'victim'** because we are hurt by their ungrateful behaviour and hurt that things have not changed.

When we rescue our teenage children, we are in fact not helping them we are disempowering them. We are taking away their own resources to think, feel and do for themselves.

Our children may well then grow up into needy adults, or adults that expect everyone else to sort out their problems for them.

To rescue a plutonian is stunting his/her growth, we are not teaching them problem solving skills.

> A teenager is someone who can hear a song by Madonna played three blocks way but not her mother calling from the next room!

However, if we move on to the 'Winners Triangle:

WINNERS TRIANGLE

ASSERTIVE

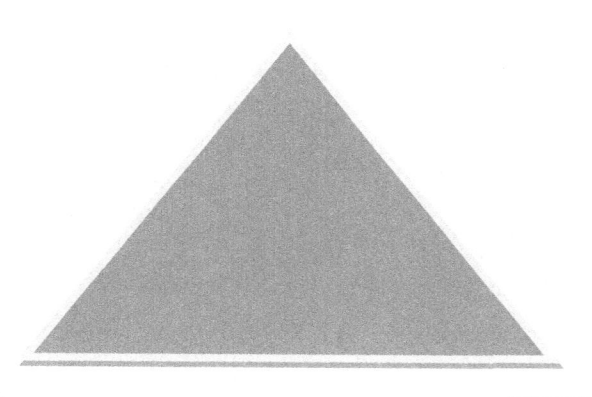

CARER   VULNERABLE

There is no shift as this is the healthy triangle.

Often parents say "I know I run around after my kids, but I don't want to stop caring for him/her". **Well, you don't have to!** Imagine this:

Think about the same or a similar scenario as the one above. Your teenager has a problem, s/he does his/her usual rant and you say:

"It's clear you have a problem Claire what might you need to do about this?"

Or

"I can see you are upset about this what are you going to do about it and how can I support you in your decision? "

(Needless to say we all communicate differently, so you may find a way to say this in a different way, however meaning the same).

The important thing is that you don't dive into rescuing. You are asking him/her what they need to do about <u>their</u> problem. What you are actually doing is empowering your teenager to take responsibility for his or her problem and to think about possible solutions.

At first your plutonian may stamp their feet and rebel against this change in you, let's face it you have been wiping their backside for them for a very long time, so the fact that you have not jumped into your normal pattern of responding will be a shock.

Stick with it, change does not always happen immediately, but it will. If they say "I don't know what I am going to do" then offer to brainstorm ideas with him/her.

But don't do it for him/her!

Look back on the scenario above and how this may have turned out differently.

> You have said one of the above statements to your child:
>
> **S/he may respond**
>
> "Well if I had some boots it wouldn't be such a problem"
>
> or
>
> "Could you take me to school, so that I don't get too wet?"
>
> or
>
> "Could you perhaps take me to the bus stop?"
>
> or
>
> "Maybe I can ask Johnny's parents to pick me up on route if it is raining"
>
> **To which you could respond:**
>
> "Yes, I am happy to do that however would you clean your room tonight when you get in as that would support me too."

Of course in answer one and two they are still asking for your help and you do have the choice to say yes or no and if it is no then it needs to be said in a firm way with no opportunity for them to try to change your mind. If you say yes, you could use this opportunity to ask them to meet you on a compromise.

By empowering your child to think for himself you are preparing him/her for adulthood and to survive independently without you.

Also, and just as importantly, you have:

1. Not jumped into rescuing
2. Not used up too much of your own time and energy but still been supporting and caring
3. Not left yourself open to resentment, anger or hurt.
4. And last but not least empowered your teenager to think, feel and do for himself.

> Some people will try to blow your candle out to make theirs shine brighter. Don't let them! Surround yourself with heart lifters NOT heart sinkers

Chapter Seven

Get off that stage!

> Raj had been talking on the phone for about half an hour before he hung up. His father said, "Wow! That was short. You usually talk for an hour. What happened?"
>
> Raj replied, "It was a wrong number."

Sigmond Freud called the teenage years 'the genital stage. Ericson called this stage of development 'the identity versus confusion' or 'intimacy versus isolation' stage. I call it the 'Drama Stage' or the 'Narcissistic Stage'.

The word 'narcissism comes from the Greek myth of Narcissus. Narcissus was a handsome Greek youth who rejected the advances of beautiful women to gaze at his own reflection in a pool of water, falling in love with himself.

In psychology, the term is used to describe both normal self love and unhealthy self absorption.

Plutonians do seem to become very absorbed in their selves at this stage of development. Do you notice this with your plutonian?

They'll even think this book is about them!

It is interesting that we say 'Stage' because from our experience it can feel like our children are on a stage. They are the prima donna and the rest of us are sitting in the wings waiting for him or her to make their demands.

I must say at this point that although I don't like to gender differentiate, it does appear that girls are worse for this than boys. At this stage of development everything is HUGE!

It is a period of life where children over catastrophes'. The hill becomes a mountain. Everything is a matter of life or death and their whole world has to revolve around them.

It can feel at times that they are moving from one drama to another, and it is very easy to get caught up in it, it can be simple, and often 'out of awareness' to find yourself on that stage with them and before you know it you are in the middle of their drama.

If you can, avoid this like the plague because there will be only one outcome. YOU will be the one that gets the blame.

Remember that this is the 'drama stage.' It is there drama not yours!

You will see evidence of this 'drama' if you have any plutonians as a friend on your face book.

When they write on their status something along the lines of "on my way to school" they get around three to six comments. If they write something negative about another plutonian or make a comment like "I hate my life!" then lo and behold they will have something in the region of fifty to one hundred comments, a thousand emojis and all asking what's up?

Who's getting the attention now?

All the other plutonians want a piece of the action; they want to join them on the stage.

Plutonians feed off drama and it is a stage of growth where they often will create a drama if there is not one going on at that time.

When your plutonian is being dramatic, making mountains out of molehills then you will be helping them by staying calm, not stepping on their stage and reality testing things with them. Also recognise that there is always a reason behind their behaviour, this would tell me that their 'self esteem bubble' is a little low. So think of ways in which you may raise their self esteem.

A plutonian can also be very "me, me, me" and they believe that they are the only one that matters in this world.

This is your opportunity to teach them that the world does not exist around them. There are other people in the family, the world too.

It is extremely important that if there are other children in the household that they do not get left in the wings whilst your plutonian is filling the stage. Make time for them too.

If there are younger siblings then they will learn from this experience too, they will know exactly what is acceptable in your home and what is not, this is preparation for the time when they reach adolescence too.

So why can teens become such drama queens. Maybe you remember your own social life in your mid teens as dynamic and, most of all, dramatic. Why? Does drama serve a purpose?

It must be exhausting for plutonians to maintain friendships in this way, so why do they have and need all this drama? Is there something good in this behaviour?

I will attempt to enlighten you. Adolescence is considered a very sensitive period for the development of social skills and social competence. One of the most important activities for our little plutonians is forming and maintaining friendships with other plutonians.

They need these relationships to form an identity and building self esteem (don't forget they are a planet and are still learning).

The plutonian brain undergoes tremendous changes related to the development of social behaviour relating to interactions with their peers, they have to learn new perspectives and understanding of the intentions of others. Their brains have to mature to reach a point of behavioural regulation.

So they have to learn on this new earth plane that to be a Martian or a Venetian they have to learn more social norms and how to adapt quickly to different social situations. Think about it they have been going to school each day for the last six or seven years to the same classroom, the same teacher and often the same classmates. Now they are being sent to a school where they have to navigate to different classrooms for different lessons, with different teachers and different classmates.

So, as they make their way towards Martians and Venetians they probably do need all the drama within their peer group in order to form their identity and to learn how to behave and feel comfortable in different social situations. They are in fight, flight or freeze as they are unsure of their environment and the drama is a consequence of this.

When 'feelings' are of a high voltage and emotions overwhelming people 'act out' – this is what they are doing.

So how you can help.

TAKE THE SPOTLIGHT OFF YOUR PLUTONIAN!!!

In the drama of your teenager's life, you have not only become the director, but the producer, the stage manager, the dresser, the caterer, the financer, the scriptwriter, the editor etc. You must be exhausted!!!

THIS SHOW IS NOW OVER!

A NEW PRODUCTION IS NOW NEEDED!

YOU ARE THE STAR NOW!

Embrace your new role and help your plutonian to manage their feelings. Teach them some emotional regulation tools. Teach them that drama's just make everything worse, and teach them to 'step off the stage.'

CHANGE IS HARD:

If you have been an enabling/rescuing parent, it will be difficult to change. However our focus is on helping the parent to change their own behaviours and responses, not those of the child.

If you have been climbing on that stage with them, getting caught up in the dramas, now is the time for change.

Change is needed to stop the pain, stop the excuses and come to a resolution.

We need to stop trying to change their behaviour by making choices/excuses for them and by shielding them from the painful consequences of their actions or inaction.

We cannot change others we can only change ourselves. We cannot change them we can only change ourselves.

You can't change someone else, but you can change your response to them. This then invites a different response from them, and they may respond this way and change.

Be warned that our children did not get this way overnight, so they won't change overnight – However as we start to change our behaviours, change will happen more quickly when we are not enabling.

We need to set boundaries!

> A teenager is a person who is always late for dinner but always on time for a rock concert.

Now for the good news:

As a parent of teenagers, it is not always about being the 'big bad wolf.'

Although consequences can change behaviour it does not always change attitude, to focus too much on negative consequences can in fact create the opposite and produce further bad behaviour, or the behaviour change may only be short lived.

Unless you use negative consequences with equally powerful positive reinforcement then you may be likely to increase the misbehaviour.

It is the positive reinforcement that produces long term attitudinal change, because when they are rewarded for their good behaviour, then this will increase and their bad behaviour will decrease. This facilitates a move into adulthood where they behave properly because they want to not because they are forced to.

It is really important that when you are trying to facilitate good behaviour to positively reinforce even the smallest of actions by your plutonian, like Martians and Venetians they love praise and the more that we are praised the more that we are likely to repeat this good behaviour.

However, don't praise their drama, praise the way in which they have dealt with the drama when they have dealt with it appropriately. Praise them when they have learned to 'step off' other plutonians drama's too.

> Remember to stay with the still waters, rather than run with the thunderstorm

Chapter Eight

Protect your inner child!

> Teenager to his friend: "Ha! My mother never saw the irony in calling me a son of a bitch!"

This is the most important chapter in the book and with this chapter alone if you practice the technique you will see massive changes in your plutonians behaviour.

However it is not the plutonian that is about to change, it is you!

So believe it or not that will be a doddle compared to trying to change a stubborn, rebellious, and dramatic plutonian!

But your change will facilitate their change.

Plutonians have a very special weapon, a very unique talent and that is the ability to 'hook into' the Martian and Venetian's emotions.

Don't forget that they have been living amongst us for the last twelve plus years; they know exactly what makes you crumple, angry and hurt.

They also know how to manipulate you too, to get their own needs met!

They make it their life's work to learn just exactly what makes you tick!

They know how to play one of you off against the other, and they also know exactly, (and this is the important part and the most dangerous), how to hook into your 'inner child.'

This is the part of us that is most vulnerable. Once they have hooked into this, then for them they have won the battle.

They know when, where and how to play up and that is because they have had years of practice.

You, however are just learning, this is possibly the first time you have had a plutonian live with you, and even if it is not they are all different from each other.

So, what do we do?

The idea is for you to change; our weapon is the ability to change, to adapt to a new way of being.

It is no good fighting fire with fire, what you need to do is to confuse him or her and the only way that you will be able to do that is by changing your own modus operands!

And we have just the tool to help you to do that:

This is the Martian's and Venetian's secret weapon.

It is a tool that I found helpful when dealing with teenagers, and enforces me to remain the parent and not the child in the relationship.

> The hardest part about
> raising teenagers
> is trying to respond
> to their behavior
> like a grown up.
>
> Playdates on Fridays

It prevents the plutonian from hooking into my emotions, and helps me to stay calm and in control.

A plutonian, by the way gets great satisfaction in seeing you out of control.

So are you ready to hear about our secret weapon?

Our secret weapon is the 'ego-state model' which came again from transactional analysis founded by Eric Berne.

Transaction analysis is an analysis of our own transactions and explore why sometimes they cause more problems than good. So a helpful tool to manage our transactions with our plutonians.

The theory of transactional analysis is that we all have three parts which Eric Berne calls ego states. We have a parent ego-state, an adult ego state and a child ego state.

This is the diagram of the ego state model, which is the secret weapon that we can use to confuse our teenagers.

Ego state model

P

A

C

Eric Berne believes that we move in and out of these states during our daily lives and during various situations, feelings and thoughts. (Different transactions)

Up until now this has probably been 'out of your awareness', however learning about ego-states enables us to bring this into 'our awareness', which can help you to form healthier relationships and think and behave in healthy ways.

And more importantly help you to manage your relationship with your plutonian more constructively.

We have possibly all experienced those times where we have been that frustrated and angry with our teenagers behaviour that we have 'lost it' with them, shouted and screamed at them, and then felt awful afterwards.

It can leave us feeling that we have lost control and to lose control with a plutonian leaves them feeling a sense of achievement, they have scored points and the one with the most points goes up in the hierarchy with their fellow plutonian. It increases their 'street cred!'

So let's learn how to manage this differently:

During any transaction when we are in our parent ego state, we feel, think and behave as our own parents or caretakers did.

This is where our transactions could be critical or nurturing, both externally and internally.

When we are in our child ego state we feel, think and behave as we did as children, although sometimes in a more adult way.

This is the state we may be in when our transactions are sulky and argumentative.

However, when we are in our adult ego state we behave in a more constructive fashion.

This is when we do our reality testing and logical thinking. In adult we deal with situations in the 'here and now' without letting past or future issues cloud our judgement.

It will be helpful if you and your partner spend some time analysing which ego state that you are in at different times of the day and in different situations. This brings you to more awareness of ego states, and yes sometimes in your communications with each other, one or the other of you will go into 'child ego state', by sulking, or fluttering your eyelashes or lashing out.

You can have some fun in analysing each other, you may get it wrong but that is okay. (But keep it secret from your plutonian, the less they know the better, you can teach it to them when they become a Martian or Venetian).

One of the common mistakes when people are doing this work is to confuse their parent ego state with their adult. That is okay it takes a while and the important thing is that when dealing with your plutonian you stay in your adult or parent and stay well away from your child ego state, unless hanging out with them and having some fun, of course.

The more that you practice and incorporate this into your daily lives, the better at it you will become. Remember all ego states are healthy when in the right one at the right time.

To help you along the way, here are a few tips:

CHILD EGO STATE is when we are hurting, sulking, fighting, arguing, or hurting other people.

It is when we are throwing tantrums, slamming doors, acting the goat, playing psychological games, or being the victim.

It is when we are unassertive, have a low self-esteem, embarrassed, feeling good, silly, and bad, bullying, teasing and joking. It is all the things we did, as children so be it sometimes in an adult way.

This is the ego-state that a plutonian will try to hook, it is where you carry all your own emotions, and the minute that they hook into this, you have lost the battle! Because you will more than likely throw a tantrum just as you did as a kid or lose control.

The plutonian will love this and consider it as 'winning'. This is the ego state that you need to leave inside of you when dealing with a stroppy plutonian.

PARENT EGO STATE is when we are scolding, criticising, praising, dictating, persecuting, teaching, nursing or nurturing self and others.

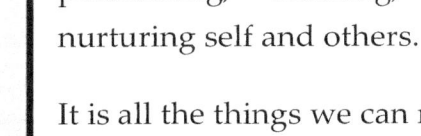

It is all the things we can remember our own caretakers doing. Remember that we will have a critical parent and a positive parent. This can be internally or externally. Be mindful that our dictating parent ego state can come out too when in conflict with our plutonian, so that's not helpful either.

We do have to be in our parent ego state when nurturing, setting clear boundaries and consequences.

So the most important ego state for all conflict in your life but particularly when in conflict with your plutonian

ADULT EGO STATE is when we are calm, rational, thinking logically and reality testing.

It is when we deal with our own and others emotions constructively.

It is when we are comfortable, okay, non judgmental accepting and honest. It is the ego state we often try to stay in, in our work environment.

The adult ego state is the ego state that helps you to manage our negative feelings of frustration and anger and prevents us from acting out our negative emotions. The adult ego state is non- threatening.

When dealing with a plutonian if we can manage to shift our self into the right ego state (which plutonians don't like either by the way) then we will be able to handle things such as our own feelings, fears and behaviour in a much more constructive way.

I must emphasise stay out of your child ego state!

A teenager is a whiz who can operate the latest computer without a lesson but can't make a bed!

Linda Mather [TEENAGERS ARE FROM PLUTO]

When communicating with your teenager the following diagram is the unhealthy position to be in!

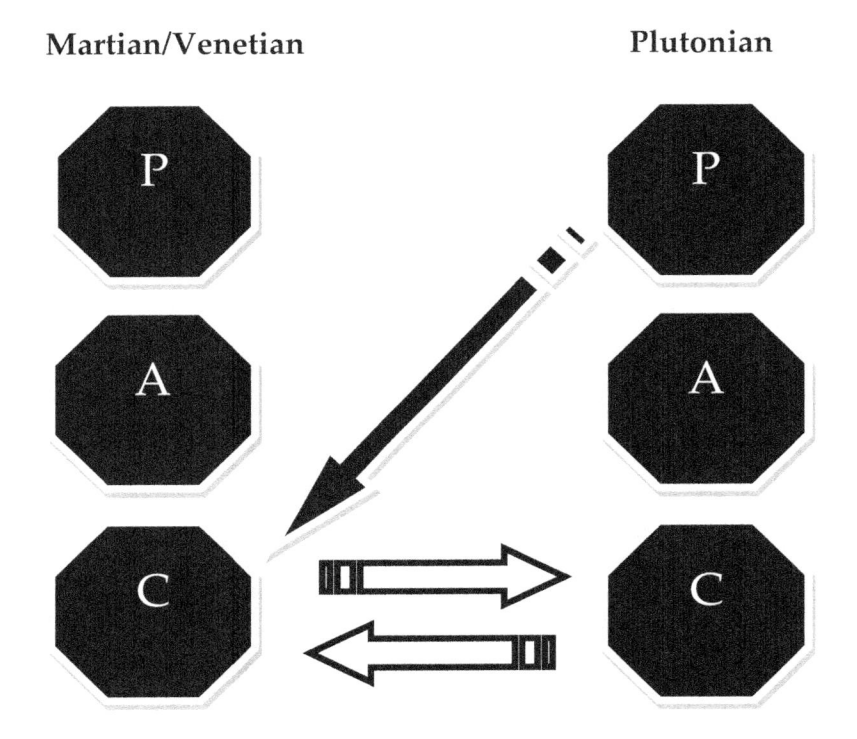

Martian/Venetian **Plutonian**

BLACK ARROW - This is the position where the teenager is hooking into your child from his or her parent ego state. An example of that is:

Plutonian: "Mum, you're not going out in that!" or "Dad you are doing that all wrong" **(Parent ego state)**

Venetian: "What should I wear then, what's wrong with it, should I go and change?" **(child ego state)**

Martian: "Why am I? If you can do it better than do it yourself!" **(child ego state)**

It is the position when your teenager is condescending towards you. His parent ego state is talking to your child ego state. It makes sense that this is not going to instigate a transaction that is helpful for either of you.

WHITE ARROWS - The other interaction (the arrows are both pointing in the direction of each other's child ego state) is when both of you are in child ego state, and communicating on a childish level.

An example of that is:

Plutonian: "It's not fair, I always have to tidy my room and what do you have to do?" **(child ego state)**

Martian: "Well, I have to do all the cleaning and the cooking (so there)" **(child ego state)**

Venetian: "It's none of your business what I have to do (nah, nah, nah, na na)" **(child ego state)**

None of these interactions are helpful to either you are your teenager, when you are in conflict.

Where do they actually get you, other than a battle of the wills?

An argument is bound to follow this kind of interaction, and as I am sure that you are aware by now that plutonians suck out of you your energy. What you may not be aware of is that in arguments with them they go out of their way to drain you of more energy. This then gives them an overflow of energy to stay up all night until depleted to then sleep all day!

One thing that you need is a bountiful of energy when raising teenagers, so the more that you can conserve the better you will feel and be able to manage other life events whilst surviving the teenage years.

This model helps you to hang on to your energy, and this will frustrate them as they cannot get at yours anymore. So they will not have the overflow and will sleep when they should at night!

> A teenager is a person who receives his allowance on a Monday, spends it on a Tuesday and borrows off you on a Wednesday.

Be aware that a plutonian will try to hook your child ego state from both his/her parent ego state or his/her own child ego state.

The idea is <u>NOT TO LET HIM!</u>

Now let's look at this change we talked about, the secret weapon of change. The weapon that will stop the plutonian from hooking into our inner child, and taking our energy ultimately stopping us from "losing it!"

The following diagram is the healthy position to be in when interacting with your plutonian:

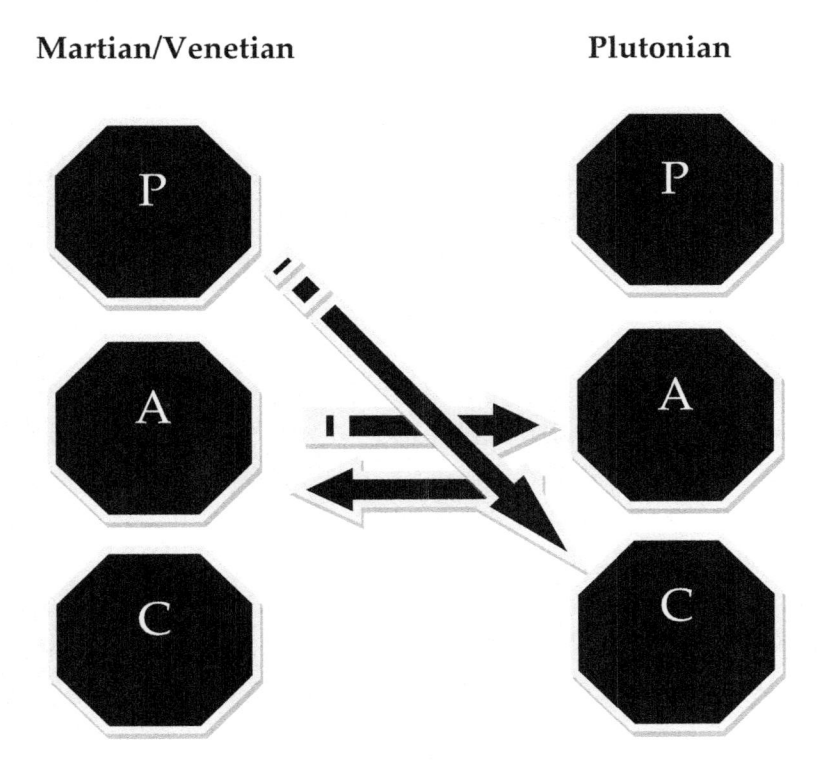

Martian/Venetian **Plutonian**

This is when you are the parent to your child, not the other way around and where you are encouraging your stroppy teenager to interact on an adult level.

Let's use the above examples again only this time interacting from one of the above positions:

Plutonian: "Mum, you're not going out in that!" or "Dad you are doing that all wrong" **(Parent ego state)**

Martian: "Can I please remind you, that you are not my husband you are my child" **(Parent ego state)**

Venetian: "How about we do it together then and you can show me the correct way" **(Adult ego state)**

And

Plutonian: "It's not fair, I always have to tidy my room and what do you have to do?"

Martian: "Would you go and tidy your room please?" **(Adult ego state)**

Venetian: "Go up the stairs and tidy your room, as you were told" **(Parent ego state)**

Can you see the difference in interactions?

The idea is not to let the Plutonian hook into the 'child' part of you that is vulnerable, and may lead you to react in a way that is not going to get you the respect that you need from your teenager.

If you 'lose it' with your child then s/he has hooked into your own child ego state.

This takes some practice and you may, especially when tired, ill, or premenopausal, fall back into old pattern. If this happens then that is okay you just make the switch there and then and start again.

Just one other point I need to reiterate is that to be in any of these ego states is healthy when you are in them at the right time. For example you and your plutonian can both be in child ego state when you are having a playful water fight or similar.

Linda Mather **[TEENAGERS ARE FROM PLUTO]**

> For the last nine million years teenagers have had just one guiding philosophy and it is greed – "Mine! Mine! Mine!"

Chapter Nine

Empathy, you've got to be kidding

> Teddy the teenager came thundering down the stairs, much to his father's annoyance.
>
> "Teddy,' he called, 'how many more times have I got to tell you to come down the stairs quietly? Now, go back up and come down like a civilised human being."
>
> There was a silence, and Teddy reappeared in the front room.
>
> "That's better," said his father. "Now will you always come down stairs like that?"
>
> "Suits me," said Teddy. "I slid down the banister."

There is one thing a plutonian hasn't got for Martians and Venetians, but they have loads of it for their friends and that is:

Empathy

Empathy is being able to step in someone else's shoes and feel what they are feeling. Would we want their sweaty feet in our shoes I ask?

There is absolutely NO POINT telling them how their behaviour makes you feel. They will just look at you as if <u>you</u> have just dropped off another planet.

They are not interested in how you feel!

To feel what we are feeling due to their behaviours would just resurrect another feeling for them and that would be "GUILT," it's not our job to make them feel guilty, it's there's to make us!

If you tell them how you feel they look at you blankly as if Martians and Venetians don't get ill, don't get upset or 'feel.' They may even say "You shouldn't feel that you are a Martian/Venetian!"

At first during my investigations, I thought that it was just something that they did not develop until they were older, but then I read their social network status and whenever another plutonian put on their site that they were unhappy, angry, hurt or any other strong feeling, they were inundated with undying support from their fellow plutonians.

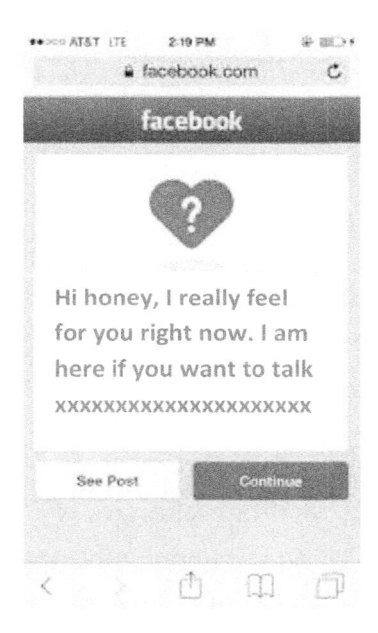

[Facebook notification image showing: "Hi honey, I really feel for you right now. I am here if you want to talk xxxxxxxxxxxxxxxxxxxxx" with See Post and Continue buttons]

They have empathy then.

When a plutonian wants their mate to stay because he is unhappy at home, they understand exactly how that mate is feeling.

So I concurred that they did have empathy, they just did not have empathy for Martians and Venetians. Why was that?

I discovered that when we said things like

"I was worried when you didn't come home last night!" or

"It really hurts when you behave in this way"

They didn't want to know because it left them feeling guilty and although a plutonian loves to make us feel guilty, they don't like feeling that way themselves.

When a plutonian has a negative feeling, to deal with this they act out in negative ways. So if s/he is feeling guilty they may act out more negatively.

Telling a plutonian how their behaviour leaves us feeling does not facilitate change; it can actually increase their poor behaviour. Especially when they are upset with you, they will do all that they can to make Martians and Venetians feel as bad as they do.

Talk to each other about how you are feeling, but don't waste your breath talking to a plutonian.

Tears from a Martian or Venetian have no effect either, if you cry because of your plutonian's behaviour, they don't know how to deal with it, so they may laugh or walk away, leaving you feeling that they do not care. They do care they have not yet learned how to show it to Martians and Venetians only to plutonians.

What you may try and this only works if you have a plutonian that is willing to do this, ask the plutonian to step into your shoes by saying something like this:

"If I went out and didn't come home, how would this leave you feeling?"

OR

"If this was your child and he never came home from school until seven o'clock how would you feel?"

If your plutonian is able to feel what you are feeling using this method, you can extend on this and say:

"So you would feel worried, so what consequence would you give out to me or your child?" OR "What response would you like to hear from me or your child to your worries?"

Then whatever s/he says, you can then say "Okay, you've chosen your own consequence for your behaviour" or "So what might you like to say to me?"

They will be confused for a couple of minutes but by the time they click on you will have left the room. Remember that reverse psychology often confuses plutonians and works marvellously to get them to agree to something.

Reverse psychology often works when trying to get them to do something they don't like to do. For example, Plutonins do not like to 'hang out' with Martians and Venetians we embarrass them! Martians and Venetians seem to say or do things that make the plutonian cringe!

You rarely see a plutonian walking outside of the house with a Martian or a Venetian, and it can be safely said that no plutonian in his or her right mind wants to be seen in public with their Martian or Venetian parents.

Even if you tell jokes like Dawn French or Michael Mckintyre, your plutonian will never crack a smile. Whatever you say and whatever you do will be a major embarrassment to them.

Dad Dancing.

Also what is worth a mention is that if you are ill in bed, don't rely on a plutonian to check in on you, bring you food or drink. If you do then be prepared to die of dehydration!

One of my plutonians did this, and when I asked why, her response was "Well you're my mum; you're not supposed to be ill!" Which confirms my point made earlier in the book, that they don't think we are human!

Another thing to be prepared for is when they get a job. You will need to stand together in battle dress when broaching the subject of a plutonian paying board; one of the funniest from one of mine was,

"I'm not paying to live in MY own house!"

And last but not least 'Boy/girlfriends' if you don't like who they are dating, DON'T TELL THEM! The more you don't like their choice of partner, the longer they will stay with them, even if THEY don't like them.

Use reverse psychology again and say you think they are wonderful and invite them round for dinner and board games. They will without a doubt dump them immediately and go out to find someone that they think you don't like. Likewise if you do like their choice of partner, tell them you don't, they will probably end up marrying them. They will certainly bring them around every night to irritate you.

A plutonian loves to aggravate you, they love to do things, see people and go places that you disapprove of, so use reverse psychology every time!

With a plutonian we have to be cleverer than they are, we have to be two steps ahead of them and we have to know what they are doing before they do.

Having said all this, it does not apply to all plutonians. I have met some that have a lot of empathy for their parents. Talking of EMPATHY, we also felt it important to talk about your empathy for them.

Often when our teenagers are behaving very badly and we dislike them immensely (still love them), we can lose empathy for them. We can feel like giving up on them completely.

This is quite normal so don't worry about it too much, however it can increase the problems within your family, because a plutonian will play up more if s/he is feeling unloved.

What usually helps is that you take some 'time out' of course and then go through some old photographs of when your plutonian was a beautiful baby, then toddler and reminisce.

By the time kids become plutonians, they know so much about their parents they use all possible tactics to make them do what they want. By that stage they have tried so many things they know what they need to say to win in a plutonian – Martian/Venetian battle.

It is not surprising, though, that the better the relationship between the two, the less likely it is that the plutonian will use these tactics, so therefore if we can develop empathy for them this will help.

For anyone that has read Men are from Mars and Women are from Venus you will know that Martians and Venetians do not have a shared language.

They speak in different languages that is hard to understand.

The same applies to plutonians, they like us say one thing and mean another, so I thought I would translate some of their common expressions for you.

Become familiar with these expressions and before you lose it, focus on the real interpretation of what you hear. You will be surprised when you do so that instead of feeling angry and frustrated, you will feel understanding and supportive and you will smile with love.

Remember when a plutonian says one thing he means another thing, here goes:

What a plutonian says:	What a plutonian means:
I am bored	I need your help. I don't know what to do with myself
I hate you!	I need you to tell me you love me
I hate school!	School was hard for me today or problems at school
I can do whatever I want!	I feel helpless and out of control
You never give me what I want!	I need something from you and it is hard for me to convince you.
No-one loves me in this family	I am looking for some attention

Linda Mather [TEENAGERS ARE FROM PLUTO]

I'm going to run away	I am afraid of running away
You don't care about me!	I need you to tell me you care about me
You are not m real mum/dad	I miss my real mum/dad and I'm having trouble adjusting to your style
All the other kids get to go and I don't!	It is hard to be different
I don't have to listen to you	I am upset that I need to listen to you
I am going to kill myself	Please help me I do not want to hurt myself
You are cruel	Tell me you love me
You never let me do anything I want	I am frustrated
Why do I have to be so different	I need the approval of my friends and it's hard when I am different from them
I don't need you	I need you so much I feel helpless
I wish you would die	Say something nice to me quick
I am not going to stay in this house	I am afraid of leaving this house
This life is not worth living	I need your help in finding the meaning in life
Its all your fault	I feel guilty

There is only one answer to all these expressions and that is:

I love you too!

This will increase your empathy and your tolerance and empower you to battle on.

A model of therapy that therapists use with children and adolescents is 'play therapy' – this is because play bypasses our defences, and also is a gateway to our unconscious. Things may come out that are more congruent than they may say in conversation.

How many times have you tried to talk with your plutonian about a problem without success? The words just don't seem to reach the plutonian. Play targets the medium of communication, it is the language of children and adolescents, it is a way in which adolescents can safely talk about their experiences, feelings and integrate themselves into the world. It helps plutonians to problem solve, think of board games for example Monopoly or Cluedo, they are both problem solving games.

Play improves relationships and is a great trust builder, you will be surprised after a few hours of fun how much you plutonian will talk to you about.

A famous quote from Plato said "You can discover more about a person in an hour of play than in a year of conversation"

> It is strong people who have the courage to show their vulnerability

Chapter Ten

Putting your learning into action!

> One day a little girl was sitting and watching her mother do the dishes at the kitchen sink. She suddenly noticed that her mother had several strands of white hair sticking out in contrast on her brunette head. She looked at her mother and inquisitively asked, "Why are some of your hairs white, Mom?"
>
> Her mother replied, "Well, every time that you do something wrong and make me cry or unhappy, one of my hairs turns white."
>
> The little girl thought about this revelation for a while and then said, "Momma, how come ALL of grandma's hairs are white?"

Finally we need a plan for if they rebel and ignore your new house rules! Remember that you are making the changes not them. The following will help you in doing this:

Developing an action plan:

It is okay to state your wish for their future, but their future is ultimately their choice, and no amount of nagging will make them change their choices.

Be clear about the changes that you are making

Don't point fingers, and try not to say "you" too much.

Tell your teenager that you've made a U-Turn and that you are changing and there is no going back.

It's okay to tell them that you have been enabling (rescuing)

Define consequences for every item on your list; you might want to consider issues around rent, laundry, curfew, zero tolerance for drugs/alcohol, food, debt, getting up in the morning, homework, chores etc.

Tell them what you are willing to do to support them.

Remain consistent, love them and follow up on all consequences

Tell them what you will not do i.e. state that you will not give them money, you will not argue or negotiate, you will not make excuses, you will not pay debts/fines, you will not accept blame.

Develop a list of resources for your adult child if they have problems eg: details of drug/alcohol treatment agencies, useful numbers to call, self help groups, books, debt counsellors, student services, counselling etc.

Planning

Develop a written plan with your partner that clearly indicates your goals. It will help you to review where you are and where you want to go.

This plan will be spoken with love and not in heated anger or frustration – it will help you to be objective

You are bringing this plan to the judgement table, not the negotiating table

You are the adult and this is your home, your money, your livelihood and your future and the time has come for you to define acceptable boundaries and to commit to them.

Presenting your action plan:

Find the right time to have the discussion

Present it with a concern for their long term wellbeing but try not to get overly emotional

Type it up if possible – make it like a formal business contract and if you can, get them to sign it

Don't present it as changes that they need to make, don't say "you need to do this". As the parent making the behaviour changes you need to inform your teenager that YOU have had a problem and therefore YOU are changing the way that you respond and behave. They can choose to change their behaviour – or not

Remember, you can't MAKE them tidy their room, but you can stop paying their mobile phone bill for example.

Don't use the word "but" – contracts don't have escape clauses

Consider the consequences – they will find it difficult, it might be hard for you to watch them hurt. However this is part of the process and they have to get desperate enough to make changes.

Ask someone for support if you need it.

Don't be surprised if it is met with resistance – this is the sign that you are doing the right thing

When they are ready to fly the nest:

Develop a transition care package – be careful about this part as we don't want to give them too much or do things on their behalf.

However there may be some instances where some additional help might make this transition easier e.g: If you ask them to move out, you may want to give them supermarket coupons, or a pre-pay phone card, or some household items etc. You should also give them important documents like birth certificates, medical history etc.

Perhaps do them a 'first aid kit' for them containing plasters, cream, bandages, headache tablets etc. Or for the new home – washing powder, cleaning materials, easy meals, cereals etc and Dad could join in for putting together their first tool box.

Make the transition as smooth as possible and yes you will shed some tears but you have done a good job to get them this far.

> Remember that you can't possibly hit the ball if you are thinking of all the possible ways you can miss.

Epilogue
Contract to take care of self

> Teenager: "My parents say that I watch too much television and that I should read more, so I turned the sub titles on!"

It is very important when raising a plutonian that you take care of <u>you</u>, and as a couple to take care of each other. When things get 'hot' take some time out. Take some deep breaths and time out.

If you can manage to give each other time out each week whilst the other one takes over that would be really good. Even of it is just for a nice quiet soak in the bath, then retire to a room, put a 'do not disturb sign' on the door and get away for a while. The plutonian will want to 'disturb' that word means nothing to them, but protect each other and tell the plutonian that you are off duty for a while and to 'pester' the other parent if they want something.

There are six steps to sanity when parenting a plutonian they are as follows:

Linda Mather [TEENAGERS ARE FROM PLUTO]

Stop your own negative behaviour such has giving in, arguing back with them, people pleasing them and meeting their needs to keep the peace!

Assemble support. – Have a good support network around you, some where you can go to have time out and someone you can talk to, maybe a therapist!

Nip excuses in the bud. Don't accept feeble excuses from your offspring for their behaviour. It is not acceptable full stop! Don't you excuse their behaviour either!

Implement rules and boundaries and stick with them. If they break those rules then dish out some consequences that you are able to follow up.

Trust your instincts. Listen to your gut, that is usually always right and you are usually right

Yield. Learn to let go of what you can't change.

> A teenager is always too tired to hold a dishcloth, but never too tired to hold a phone!

I hope the tools in this book have been helpful; they will only work though if you use them. It might be about you and your partner sitting down and making a commitment to each other and yourselves to take action. This involves the following;

Making a commitment contract to yourself

I shall take care of my own spiritual, mental, physical, emotional and financial health

I shall remember to express love and attention to my partner and other family member and friends in addition to my troubled teenage child

I shall not accept excuses

I shall understand that a clear definition of right and wrong is imperative

I shall make fact based judgements without excuse or feeling guilty

I shall uphold standards of behaviour that protect my morals, values and integrity

Linda Mather [TEENAGERS ARE FROM PLUTO]

I shall give my teenager unconditional love and support without meddling and without money

I shall celebrate life and love as often as possible even in times of trouble

I shall define my goals as they relate to my life, not to the life of my teenager

I shall make my decisions based on long term   goals, not short terms remedies; and act accordingly

.... signed Venetian

....................................signed Martian

That is your first commitment to stopping this enabling pattern

Better to do it in "one fell swoop" rather than dragging it out. Dragging it out sends mixed messages to our teenagers and it is hard on us as parents to volley back and forth between enabling behaviour and clear boundaries

Linda Mather [TEENAGERS ARE FROM PLUTO]

> Never let yesterday use up too much of today, it's never too late to be what you might have been.

And if all else fails then bide your time and as the poem says on the next page, move in with them when you are old and senile and make their lives the living hell that they made yours!

Linda Mather [TEENAGERS ARE FROM PLUTO]

I'll live with my children and bring them great joy
and repay all I've had from each girl and boy.
I will draw on the walls and scuff up the floor,
run in and run out without closing the door.

I'll hide frogs in the pantry, socks under my bed.
Whenever they scold me, I'll hang down my head.
I'll run and I'll romp, always fritter away
the time to be spent doing chores every day.

I'll pester my children when they're on the phone.
As long as they're busy I won't leave them alone.
Hide candy in closets, rocks in a drawer,
and never pick up my clothes from the floor.

Dash off to the movies and not wash a dish.
I'll plead for allowance whenever I wish.
I'll stuff up the plumbing and deluge the floor.
As soon as they've mopped it I'll flood it some more.

When they correct me, I'll lie down and cry,
kicking and screaming, not a tear in my eye.
I'll take all their pencils and flashlights and then
when they buy new ones, I'll take them again.

I'll spill glasses of milk to finish each meal,
eat my banana and just drop the peel.
Put toys on the table, spill jam on the floor.
I'll break lots of dishes as though I were four.

What fun I shall have, what joy it will be to
live with my children the way they lived with me!
Source unknown

NB:

Don't think that you are in this alone; there are many agencies out there that can support you. Check with your local social services, school or college, CAMHs or GP practice that will be aware of what help is in your area.

If your child is showing signs indicative of the following then this is when you need professional help and the above organisations will be able to signpost you to the right agency:

Substance misuse

Heavy alcohol use

Self harm

Eating disorders

Depression/anxiety

Abuse issues

Mental health issues

Or anything else that you are concerned about.

Author's words.

Who would have thought that an innocent conversation at a dinner party would have led to the formation of a new book?

A conversation about the parenting of teenagers and by the time I got home I had felt, "a new book coming on!"

I hope that this book achieves what I aimed to achieve and that was a light hearted but also a serious look at teenagers, their behaviours and some basic tips on how to adapt your parenting style to help you to overcome some of the difficulties that you may be having with your offspring.

I have been there and I just thank God that he created us so that they had bypassed that stage by the time I reached menopause or none of us would be around to tell the tale.

It does get better, and happens a lot quicker if you have the right tools to manage this difficult period of your child's life.

Linda Mather [TEENAGERS ARE FROM PLUTO]

As a final story.

I was sat on a train recently whilst on my lap top proof reading this book and making slight amendments, when an old lady came and sat next to me.

She began chatting and explained that she had been to visit her six children, eighteen grandchildren and five great grandchildren in Birmingham.

Then she enquired what I was doing.

I told her fully expecting her to question me for free professional advice.

Instead she sat back, picked up her magazine and said, "If there is anything you want to know, just ask me."

The moral of this story is listen to your own parent's advice because they have been there, wore the T shirt and swallowed the video, making their own mistakes along the way.

Hold your breath and tell yourself that it is not forever, it is only until s/he grows into a Martian or Venetian.

AND

BE WARNED IF YOU DON'T GET IT RIGHT THEY COULD STAY PLUTONIANS UNTIL THEY ARE WELL INTO THEIR 30's OR 40's!

Good Luck.

Linda Mather

FUNNY THINGS TEENAGERS SAY

"If you think the things I say out loud are bad you should hear the things that I keep to myself".

"I'm more confused than a chameleon in a bag of skittles."

"My childhood is like being drunk, everyone remembers what I did and said except me!"

"I used to think I was indecisive, but now I'm not quite sure"

"If two wrongs don't make a right, try three"

"I'm not lazy, I am on energy saving mode"

"Mum what year did we go to Holland for the Euro 2000?"

"Sorry for the mean, awful, accurate things I said"

"One advantage of talking to yourself is that you know at least someone is listening"

"Board, what do you mean board? I'm not paying to live in my own house!"

"Okay if I have to pay to live in my own house, then I'm buying all my own food and tidying my own bedroom!"

OTHER BOOKS BY LINDA MATHER:

Novels:
Gut Instinct
A woman's world
Jane, me and myself
The Haymaker

Self help books:
I shall wear purple
I shall be blue
I shall be clean

Counselling text books:
An Introduction to counselling skills and theory
Training Manual for Certificate to Diploma in therapeutic counselling
Counselling and psychotherapy training – Level 4

Children's books:
The fairy on top of the Christmas tree

Linda's previous novels

Reviews for "Gut Instinct"

Brilliant!!!,

I was engrossed right from the start. Excellent piece of writing, keeps you hanging on the whole way through! I love psychological thrillers; this is one of the best I have read in a long time! What an ending, well done, the author fantastic read!!!!

Twisted tale!

I was sucked into the story early on and spent the rest of the day reading. Easy to read, amusing, puzzling, sad, savage, insightful AND with a twist in the tale. I am looking forward to the next book.

Brillant

Well I didn't expect that at the end. I couldn't put this book down and read 30 chapters in one night. Well done on a brilliant book.

Excellent!

This is an excellent read, the author has the style of James Patterson and although a slow beginning a page turner four chapters in.

Brilliant Read!

I could not put this book down it should be turned into a film. What an ending!!!

Mindboggling!

This book is an incredible psychological thriller that has you gripped from beginning to end, and what an ending. This author is a wonderful storyteller. I would recommend it to anyone who likes thrillers to read this.

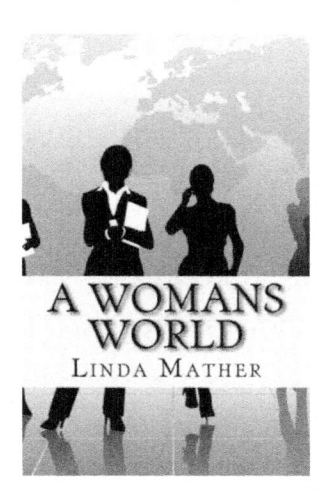

Reviews for "A woman's world"

Interesting

A thought provoking book.

Another great book!

This author has the ability to get you thinking even after you have finished the book.

Food for thought

Would the grass be greener? Would the world be a better place? This is a story that gives us insights into the alternatives and asks us 'Which world would you prefer to live in?' Linda's second novel is as easy to read as the first and just as enjoyable. I suspect the film would have plenty of scope for some interesting details.

Good Storyteller

I am impressed with your story telling abilities.

Thought provoking

This is an interesting concept; this writer has a good way of telling stories, a thought provoking book. A thoroughly enjoyable read.

Printed in Great Britain
by Amazon